LESTER SUMRALL
I PREDICT
2000
A.D.

D1716153

Unless otherwise indicated
all Scripture quotations are taken from
the *King James Version of the Bible*.

I PREDICT 2,000 A.D.
ISBN 0-937580-03-1
Copyright © 1987 by Lester Sumrall
Over 100,000 copies in print

Published by LeSEA Publishing Company
P.O. Box 12
South Bend, Indiana 46624

CONTENTS

1

I PREDICT:

THIS GENERATION IS NOT READY FOR THE 21ST CENTURY

Millions of people now living will be literally dragged, kicking and screaming into Century Twenty-one!

Man is not ready mentally, morally, or spiritually for the millennia determined upon planet Earth.

Mentally, man with all his science has not studied the unerring truth of prophecy.

Modern man has not prepared his thinking to move from the natural to the supernatural.

2000 A.D.

As planet Earth spins toward 2000 A.D.
The wizard cries aloud, "What shall be?"
The witch doctor mumbles in voice that is low,
"My spirit cannot tell the way to go."

The palm reader studies the lines of
    a man's hand
And cries, "I see no place to stand."
The spiritist cries out, "Darken the room!"
Then shouts aloud, "I see only doom."

The Christian arises with a face aglow
Holding the Bible he says, "This is the way
    to go."
With strong voice he cries, "Do not fear."
The Book declares, The Messiah is near.

The scientist says of 2000 A.D.
Star wars there will surely be.
The banker holds his millions tight
Saying, "Where can I invest that is right?"

The statesman cries out, "We need a man
    of power."
Our world has never seen such an hour.
Religion sadly responds, "We have not heard
From heaven, we have not received a word."

Western culture weeps aloud, saying,
    "Don't look at me,
I have emptied all truth into the sea."
The Christian facing 2000 A.D.
Cries to everybody, "Look and see!

"I have truth for your tomorrow
I know the way out of sorrow.
Turn to Christ, He is the Way
For 2000 A.D. is to be HIS DAY."

Satan cries, "The time is at hand
There will not be a virgin in the land.

"Abortion, abortion is the answer," he cries,
"Just have your pleasure and say, 'Goodbye.' "
Satan says, "My sweetest word is 'Sodom'
There I made man hit the bottom."

Sodomy means to grab the youth
And blind them from what is truth.
Seduce them to make love
Tell them there is no Father above.

Millions of earthdwellers facing 2000 A.D.
Cry loudly, "We desire to know what is to be!"
God answers to all who pervert the soul
The Lake of Fire is your final goal.

The Bible says that on Mt. Sinai, God spoke
   in thunder.
On the day of Pentecost, God spoke in wonder.
In the last days, He will speak by divine
   inspiration,
He will speak to the world by congregation.

He will speak clearly by the voice of hosts,
Thousands shall be led in unity by the Holy
   Ghost.
Mighty leaders of the black race shall rise,
Their eyes shall not be toward men, but
   to the skies.

Their voices in loud cry shall sound like rage,
They shall declare the termination of this age.
Before the fateful year of 2000 A.D.
   great spiritual movements shall soar,
Millions of men and women shall shout to
   Christ, "Give us more!"

As God took Gideon and his valiant 300 men,
He destroyed multitudes of men of sin.
God used young Jonathan the son of a king,
To make the loud voice of victory ring.

God smote the enemy in each generation,
He did it in battle array or by sensation.
But now by the power of His strong arm,
The devil and his followers will have alarm.

The astrologist whispers, "Just look to the stars.
There is the extragalactic nebulae and there
     is Mars."

The Ouija board speaks out to man,
"I your destiny can expand."

The witch doctor peering from his dark room,
Growls out to millions, "You will be here
     soon."

The mass media of newspaper, magazine and
     television,
Cries aloud, "Century Twenty-one will make
     its own decision."
While millions will look to the mystics of
     demon power,
They boast, "Of all times, this is our hour."

The Bible is God's prophetic story,
For thousands of years it has revealed God's
     glory.
The Bible is a strong light to show the way,
For the 2000 A.D. citizens to find the way.

The Word of God responds, "I will reveal
     the story,
Century Twenty-one is for heaven's glory."
So come, you millions, all who truth will seek,
The infallible truth is God's Word for
     the meek.

Ultimately, while angels will guide you around
    the blood of Armageddon,
Shout when the Christ is revealed from heaven.
The modern man cries, "When history's fateful
    time clock rings out 2000 A.D.,
  What kind and sort of mankind will there be?"

Will government, education and families still
    remain?
Will our neighbors and friends be the same?
Who today can turn on the light for tomorrow?
Who can beckon mankind to come out of
    sorrow?

Can sorcerers conjure up man's fate
And speak before it is too late?
Or can guru from far-off land
Speak more than writing in the sand?

Do the marvels of the science laboratory
    claim to fulfill men's final story?

There will be a strange man whose number
    is 666,
He will proclaim every human ill to fix.
He will loudly declare that sin is not sin,
And his spider's web he shall surely spin.

But Christ shall melt him in battle array,
Declaring to the universe, "This is my day!"
The day of Jesus is ahead!

2

I PREDICT:

MANY SHALL DIE OF FEAR BEFORE 2000 A.D.

I predict tormenting fear to grasp the hearts of modern men as they face 2000 A.D.

Modern man has never been so fearful of a date as he is of the year of 2000 A.D.

There are forebodings in the keenest minds. Leaders in political, social and financial empires seek to interpret what is ahead as they face the seeming mystical year of 2000 A.D.

The astrologers are as busy as they were in Pharaoh's court when Moses arrived. They are as frightened as the king and his princes were in Nebuchadnezzar's court when the finger of

God counted time and the magicians heard that Babylon's time had *run out.*

There is a deistic, demonic, and humanistic showdown speeding toward the year 2000 A.D. Planet Earth is charging toward a changing decade, a changing century, and a changing millennium!

I PREDICT FEAR TO DESTROY MILLIONS BEFORE 2000 A.D.

Today multitudes are singing the "21st Century Blues." Millions possess an innate fear of the greatest transition of society in a thousand years. Many see sinister forebodings in the approaching of the calendar year 2000 A.D.

THE GLOBAL MARCH

Fear is on a global march! The outbreak of World War I in 1914 caused the beginning of a great march of fear across the world. The economic depression of the 1930s further accelerated this vicious enemy's march. Material insecurity brought near panic to millions of hearts.

World War II produced more fear. The world advanced from rather primitive warfare. World War I—dropping small bombs from aircraft—to the atomic blasts of Nagasaki and Hiroshima at the end of World War II. All intelligent humans then realized there was no place to hide.

Since World War II, scientists and statesmen have continually predicted the impending extermination of the human race. From this fear, the United Nations was born.

Tensions, caused by devastating fear, grip the hearts of millions of frustrated people. The world is now looking for a political genius who, by bringing peace to the fearful nations, can relieve these tensions.

UNMASKING MAN'S DEADLIEST ENEMY

"There is no fear in love; but perfect love casteth out fear: because fear hath torment" (I John 4:18).

Fear has been called the Black Monster. Today this monster is striking with a demonic fury, waging aggressive warfare upon helpless people of all nations. Because of this wicked ogre, multitudes of modern lives are suffering material destruction, moral degradation, and spiritual annihilation.

The Black Monster, which torments rational

people, is not the ordinary excitement one feels after hearing a sudden noise or when performing a perilous task. This monster, unmasked, is an unreasoning, tormenting, persisting fear that makes life difficult and distressing, blacking out people's personalities with dark clouds of apprehension and hallucination.

UNIVERSAL FEAR

The problem most often presented to me by people of every color and social position throughout the world is the problem of *fear*.

In addition to religious leaders, thinking people from all other walks of life are alert to this onslaught of fear. Herbert Hoover, a former President of the United States, summarized what he learned during an official world tour. Upon his return to America, he said: "The dominant emotion everywhere in the world is *fear*. This applies to every part of human activities—finance, industry, farmers, workers, thinkers, and government officials." This painful and heart-stirring report is from a wise statesman and qualified observer.

Medical authorities also realize that the world is in the iron-clasped grip of an invisible enemy, whose unrelenting stranglehold is destroying the vital life of society. Doctors fight an increasing number of battles against this real, yet unreal, monster in their patients. They are studying more and more the mental man along with the physical man.

In the political arena, world rulers are almost to the same frustration point that King Belshazzar reached. The night his empire dissolved into the rubble of history amid the wine, women, and song of a state banquet, the Bible says, "...the king's countenance was changed...the joints of his loins were loosed, and his knees smote one against another" (Daniel 5:6).

The cause of fear in that day was the organized might of the victorious Medes and Persians. Today it is the awful blasts of atomic bombs, intercontinental missiles, germ warfare, and deadly rays from outer space. Statesmen are among those most aware that there is no place to hide.

THE FOUR FREEDOMS

During World War II, at a secret rendezvous in the Atlantic Ocean, President Roosevelt and British Prime Minister Winston Churchill drew up the historic document known as the Atlantic Charter. This modern "Magna Carta" is considered one of the greatest charters championing the common liberties of mankind. It will be remembered throughout history for its Four Freedoms: Freedom from Want, Freedom from Fear, Freedom of Speech, and Freedom of Religion.

During the most dreadful conflict of history, these statesmen listed *fear* as one of the four major evils of the world. Our modern world is enslaved by fear of war, secret police, hunger, and oppression. These allied statesmen solemnly vowed to give themselves to the fight against the Black Monster of fear.

WHO AND WHY

Fear respects no one. It haunts the unlearned and the university-educated alike. It strikes at the highborn and those of humble origin. It walks the floors of the mansion and palace as well as the floors of the hut. Men from all walks of life have failed equally in the entrusted job of building a successful and happy life—a job which prepares one to live forever with God.

FEAR AND PROPHECY

Fear has a prophetical connotation. Since the first law was broken in the Garden of Eden, human fear has always existed because it is the fruit of disobedience. However, one of the certain end signs of the present world system and the return of the Lord Jesus Christ to the earth is the many deadly, black, demonlike fears corrupting human society.

Proving from the Bible that the worldwide outbreak of fear is a prophetical sign of the end of the world as we know it, will give us an all-renewed courage to prevent fear from overwhelming us as we battle against it.

> And there shall be signs in the sun, and in the moon, and in the stars; and upon the earth distress of nations, with perplexity; the sea and the waves roaring;
>
> Men's hearts failing them for fear, and for looking after those things which are coming on the earth: for the powers of heaven shall be shaken.
>
> And then shall they see the Son of man coming in a cloud with power and great glory.
>
> And when these things begin to come to pass, then look up, and lift up your heads; for your redemption draweth nigh. (Luke 21:25-28)

Here Christ predicted cosmic disturbances in the heavens as an endtime sign. Since the time of Noah and the Flood, there have been cosmic disturbances. According to historical records, these disturbances have greatly accelerated within the last century.

The entire news media—daily newspapers, magazines, radio and television—inform us of the horrible disasters of earthquakes in many lands. They tell of tidal waves, typhoons, hurricanes, and cyclones occurring in our present day.

Christ said, "There shall be...upon the earth distress of nations, with perplexity." Could anyone describe present world conditions with better words? Yet Christ spoke these words almost 2000 years ago. He meant them as a sign to alert those living near the time of His return and the end of the world.

Jesus declared that men's hearts would be "failing them for fear, and for looking after those things which are coming on the earth."

Christ plainly predicted today's phobias. He said that men and women observing civilization's present-day circumstances would find their hearts gripped by deadly fear.

The great number of suicides among well-known industrialists in many countries today is evidence of this dreadful fear mania. Their hearts could not stand the pressure of what they could see coming upon this world.

Political leaders have suffered in a similar way. As they have observed the horizons black with national and international strife and bloodshed, their hearts have melted. The layman, without a technical knowledge of coming events, feels the very air filled with fear.

As the horrible holocaust of Armageddon slowly draws nearer, this sinful and rebellious world becomes more and more fearful.

ISAIAH'S PROPHECY

In addition to the great prophecies of Christ regarding fear in the last days, the Bible also records descriptions given by Old and New Testament prophets of the condition of men's hearts at the end of the age.

Isaiah, the greatest prophet of the Old Testament, saw the end of time and prophesied of these conditions:

> For the day of the Lord of hosts shall be upon every one that is proud and lofty, and upon every one that is lifted up; and he shall be brought low...

> And they shall go into the holes of the rocks, and into the caves of the earth, for fear of the Lord, and for the glory of his majesty, when he ariseth to shake terribly the earth.

> In that day a man shall cast his idols of silver, and his idols of gold, which they made each one for himself to worship, to the moles and to the bats;

> To go into the clefts of the rocks, and into the tops

of the ragged rocks, for fear of the Lord, and for the glory of his majesty, when he ariseth to shake terribly the earth.

Cease ye from man, whose breath is in his nostrils: for wherein is he to be accounted of?
(Isaiah 2:12, 19-22)

All students of prophecy identify the "day of the Lord of hosts" with the end of Gentile rule in world affairs. At that terrible time the proud sinners of the world, in trying to hide themselves from a righteous God, shall seek refuge in rocks and mountain hideouts.

Today nations are ready to make their abode and hiding place in the holes and rocks of the earth. This condition brings an intense fear into the hearts of mankind.

SOLOMON SAYS...

When man has run God's last red light and finds himself abandoned of a Savior, even his prayers will profit nothing.

Solomon, the wise seer of Israel, wrote these words:

I also will laugh at your calamity; I will mock when your fear cometh;

When your fear cometh as desolation, and your destruction cometh as a whirlwind; when distress and anguish cometh upon you.

Then shall they call upon me, but I will not answer;
they shall seek me early, but they shall not find
me...

But whoso hearkeneth unto me shall dwell
safely, and shall be quiet from fear of evil.
(Proverbs 1:26-28,33)

Solomon, with his God-given wisdom, saw a
time when fear, desolation, distress, and anguish would come upon mankind.

JOHN'S REVELATION

In the New Testament, John, the beloved
disciple, predicted in the Revelation that the
time would come when men and women
would hide in the holes of the earth for fear
of the things that were coming to pass. (Revelation 6:14-17)

He was prophetically previewing modern
atomic bombs, germ warfare, and cosmic rays
from outer space.

Perfect love casteth out FEAR.

3

I PREDICT:

STAR WARS BY 2000 A.D.

Star Wars used to be fiction. It was called Buck Rogers' adventures. It was a fantasy of the human brain. But today, the American military has created a Star Wars weapon.

The MX missile can strike an atomic bomb fired inside Russia while it is still in the air; it can track the bomb down like a blood hound. The MX missile has the power to intercept the enemy's bombs over his own territory so that when it explodes, it falls back into the territory where it originated.

Russia claims she has 10,000 atomic bombs and that no city in America can hide from her; yet, America's Star Wars missiles can and will immobilize the threat of Russia's atomic arsenal.

Russia would not negotiate if she did not fear the Star War weapons.

The big question in your mind and mine is, "If Russia had this capability rather than America, what would she do with that capability?"

At the conference table she is asking America to quit her Star Wars exploration, but, if Russia had this same capability, would she abandon it or would she demand the whole world to bow at her feet in abject slavery? That is the difference.

GOD'S WORD SPEAKS ABOUT STAR WARS

The book of Judges 5:20 says, "They fought from heaven; the stars in their courses fought against Sisera." Sisera was a mighty general. Judges 4:3 tells us that he had nine hundred chariots of iron. That is like having nine hundred tanks in the field today. For 20 years he had oppressed Israel. Finally, the people cried unto God and He forgave them, then God fought from heaven and the stars in their courses fought this heathen, pagan general.

It would be interesting to know exactly how the stars in their courses fought Sisera and defeated him. He had to jump out of the chariot and flee on foot.

When he met a beautiful lady who offered him a refreshing drink, he sealed his own destiny. He drank his milk and it so satisfied his belly that he lay on the ground and fell asleep.

As soon as he was unconscious, she took a long wooden nail and pinned him to the ground; the nail went right through his head.

What the Israeli army was not able to do, a cunning woman did. She smiled at General Sisera, but it was a smile of death.

THE STAR OF JUDGMENT

God can use the heavens to fight evil.

In Revelation 8:10-11, there is a star of judgment.

And the third angel sounded, and there fell a great star from heaven, burning as it were a lamp, and it fell upon the third part of the rivers, and upon the fountains of waters.

And the name of the star is called Wormwood.

The prophet said there will be a star called "Wormwood," not just MX. "And the third part of the waters became wormwood; and many men died of the waters." There is a war of the future which will be carried on by stars.

THE GUIDING STAR

There is a very exciting star that we know about.

In Matthew 2:2 we read about the "guiding star."

> Where is he that is born King of the Jews? for we have seen his star in the east, and are come to worship him.

I suppose that God could not get humans to guide men to the Savior that they might worship Him, so His stars did it. There are many functions that stars participate in. Christ is a promised star.

Numbers 24:17 says,

> I shall see him, but not now: I shall behold him, but not nigh: there shall come a Star out of Jacob, and a Sceptre shall rise out of Israel...."

Christ is that shimmering star, a star of power, a star of victory, that came out of Jacob to the world.

THE DAY STAR

We have also a more sure word of prophecy;

a light that shineth in a dark place, until the day
dawn, and the day star arise in your hearts.

(II Peter 1:19)

Christ is that eternal Star of brightness. The
day star is seen by day and by night. It shines
so brightly that in the evening time the star can
be clearly seen. Early in the morning you look
and there is that star outshining everything else
while the other stars are vanishing. This bright
shining star is called the "Morning Star." Jesus
is the day Star that has risen to shine in our
hearts.

THE MORNING STAR

It is most interesting that God has had con-
siderable to say about stars before man had his
Star Wars.

In Revelation 2:28 the Word of God says,
"And I will give him the morning star." This
is said to the overcomer.

The morning star shines brightly in the
early morning when the other stars are not
seen. God has promised us that if we are over-
comers, He is going to let us be as the morning star shining in beauty and brightness above
the other stars in the firmament. God may have
many stars, but we shall outshine them all.

THE STAR GIFT

On the last page of every Bible, Revelation 22:16 says,

I, Jesus, have sent mine angel to testify unto you these things in the churches. I am the root and the offspring of David, and the bright and morning star.

Christ is that magnificent, shining Star that forever shines.

Christ is the Star of all star wars.

SATELLITES ARE STARS

In a remarkable way, the satellites that are in the heavens are these stars. The heavens are jammed with them. There could very well be a few thousand up there right now doing all kinds of operations for man. Some of them just transmit newspapers and carry through a printing process. *The Wall Street Journal*, at the same moment it is being printed in Boston, is also printed in Atlanta. This is done by satellite. It comes out in a full page, jumps into the sky and comes back down in another city. All kinds of uses are made of these man-made stars.

A great battle for these man-made stars will be a moral battle. They have become polluted.

My wife and I were almost shocked out of our wits recently. Before retiring in our hotel room, we turned on the TV set and were confronted by the rawest sex that could ever happen. Sodom could not have been as bad as what we saw on that television. I cut it off as quickly as I could.

The next morning I went to the manager of the hotel. At first he was going to say, "Well, let everybody do as he pleases."

I said, "You have a responsibility to the public; you have a responsibility to keep filth out of here and protect your guests from the devil's work."

The devil is putting all kinds of filth in the stars. What in the world can we do about it?

If you cannot keep the bad out, put the good up there with it. At least the people have a choice. Do not fold your hands and quit; do not cease to do anything. Fight!

There is a real Star War going on and it has to do with a moral crisis. We should say, "God, give us the skies."

The greatest Star War we have is spiritual.

The Bible says that Satan is the prince and the power of the air. His headquarters is among the stars and we have authority to cast him out. We have to break him down. All the unclean spirits that fell with Lucifer out of heaven inhabit the air. We have to invade that bunch. The Church must become tired of them invading us. We must decide that it is time for us to invade them. We must start a Star Wars battle and go after the prince and the power of the air to cast him down by the blood of Jesus and the power of the Great Commission.

There is a little gospel in the satellites, but not even one percent of what is in the air is gospel. We are not covering the heavens. We have not started a big revolution up there yet. We must have a real Star War!

The biggest problem in the stars is rebellion against God. We need to start a continual war against the devil and his demons and against anything that is ungodly and unhealthy and unclean.

DESTINY IN THE SKY

The Lord spoke to me, "Your destiny is in the sky."

I said, "Oh, Lord. What do you mean?"

He replied, "Your mightiest thrust will be in the sky."

I immediately started studying television via satellites. I began praying, "God, please, give us victories up there."

On an airplane coming back from Israel, a little lady who had been sitting behind me a few seats, came up and tapped me on the shoulder. She said, "God just spoke to me and told me that He was going to have His angels clear the skies so that the gospel could get in."

About ten minutes later she came back and tapped me on the shoulder and said, "I do not think that I got through to you. God told me that He was going to have His angels clear the skies so the gospel could get in there."

If there is ever a time when we need to invade the heavens, it is now!

Through satellite, shortwave radio, television and radio, we are putting Jesus among the stars. We are putting salvation in the air. We are going to fight all the devil's work that is up there. There is going to be a Star War. We are going to fight them, in Jesus' name. We are going to tell them that the Bible says something about stars.

God cast down Sisera by the stars. He has a star that is called "Wormwood" that can destroy a third of the human race. God is engaged in Star Wars and we are on His side. We are on the winning team in the Star Wars. We have no fear of the enemy and no fear of atomic bombs.

The stars have a very remarkable part to play in the story of human destiny. Man will not destroy this earth by atomic bombs. God will determine planet Earth's destiny.

God will burn up the earth because it is polluted with sins. I continually pray that the Lord will help us to be on God's side, the side of holiness and righteousness.

4

I PREDICT:
THE SALE
OF THE SOULS OF MEN
BY 2000 A.D.

The devil, in his final onslaught against God and man, is angry because he knows his time is short. He lashes out in fury against the human race.

After this I saw another angel coming down from heaven. He had great authority, and the earth was illuminated by his splendor. With a mighty voice he shouted:

Fallen! Fallen is Babylon the Great! She has become a home for demons and a haunt for every evil spirit, a haunt for every unclean and detestable bird.

For all the nations have drunk the maddening wine of her adulteries. The kings of the earth committed adultery with her, and the merchants of the earth grew rich from her excessive luxuries.
(Revelation 18:1-3 NIV)

When the kings of the earth who committed adultery with her and shared her luxury see the smoke of her burning, they will weep and mourn over her.

Terrified at her torment, they will stand afar off and cry: Woe, Woe, O great city, O Babylon, city of power! In one hour your doom has come!

The merchants of the earth will weep and mourn over her because no one buys their cargoes any more.

Cargoes of gold, silver, precious stones and pearls; fine linen, purple, silk and scarlet cloth; every sort of citron wood, and articles of every kind made of ivory, costly wood, bronze, iron and marble;

Cargoes of cinnamon and spice, of incense, myrrh and frankincense, of wine and olive oil, of fine flour and wheat; cattle and sheep; horses and carriages; and bodies *and souls of men.*
(Revelation 18:9-13 NIV)

...By your magic spell all the nations were led astray.

In her was found the blood of prophets and of the saints, and of all who have been killed on the earth.
(Revelation 18:23-24 NIV)

"Babylon" means confusion. It represents moral and spiritual degradation.

WHAT IS BEING SOLD?

In these ultimate times, the human body is for sale.

The immortal soul is at stake.

The mind of man is bargained for in the marketplace.

The emotion of man is a victim of commerce.

The will of man is broken and sold at bargain prices.

This speaks of national bondage, of slavery and servitude to evil powers.

Babylon represents reprobated religions. It is called THE GREAT WHORE.

It speaks of prostituted religion.

And there came one of the seven angels which had the seven vials, and talked with me, saying unto me, Come hither; I will shew unto thee the judgment of the great whore that sitteth upon many waters:

With whom the kings of the earth have committed fornication, and the inhabitants of the earth have been made drunk with the wine of her fornication.

And upon her forehead was a name written, MYSTERY, BABYLON THE GREAT,

THE MOTHER OF HARLOTS AND ABOMINA-
TIONS OF THE EARTH.

And he saith unto me, The waters which thou
sawest, where the whore sitteth, are peoples, and
multitudes, and nations, and tongues.
(Revelation 17:1-2, 5, 15)

Selling human slaves has always been an evil
of wicked men. Religion can sell the souls of
men through deception. Much of what the
present-day church is teaching about the Word
of God is not valid.

Religion sells men's souls through lies, declaring that these are not the prophetical last
days.

Millions of people all over the world have
become the merchandise of religion.

Think of India where the devil has made the
people believe there are over 300,000,000
gods.

Think of the primitive lands where *fear* is a
god to be worshiped.

Christ declared a cycle of time. He chose the
days of Noah and said the earth shall be
likewise again.

But of that day and hour knoweth no man, no,
not the angels of heaven, but my Father only.

But as the days of Noe were, so shall also the coming of the Son of man be.

For as in the days that were before the flood they were eating and drinking, marrying and giving in marriage, until the day that Noe entered into the ark,

And knew not until the flood came, and took them all away; so shall also the coming of the Son of man be. (Matthew 24:36-39)

And as it was in the days of Noe, so shall it be also in the days of the Son of man. (Luke 17:26)

Which sometime were disobedient, when once the longsuffering of God waited in the days of Noah, while the ark was a-preparing, wherein few, that is eight souls were saved by water. (I Peter 3:20).

Christ determined that before His return there would be a completed cycle of the basest morals.

Men would sell their souls to evil. God warns us today that selling our souls to pagan religions and pagan practices will bring the same judgment as it did before.

Also, the Bible teaches in II Peter 2:6,

And turning the cities of Sodom and Gomorrah into ashes condemned them with an overthrow, making them an ensample unto those that after should live ungodly.

The Holy Spirit warns us in Jude verse 7,

Even as Sodom and Gomorrah, and the cities about them in like manner, giving themselves over to fornication, and going after strange flesh, are set forth for an example, suffering the vengeance of eternal fire.

The value of the human soul will go down before 2000 A.D.

Religion will make merchandise of immortal souls, deceiving and being deceived.

To be forewarned is to be forearmed.

5

I PREDICT:

THE FALL OF RUSSIA BEFORE 2000 A.D.

Abraham was called by God to be the father of the nation of Israel.

> Now the LORD said unto Abram, Get thee out of thy country, and from thy kindred, and from thy father's house, unto a land that I will shew thee:
>
> And I will make of thee a great nation, and I will bless thee and make thy name great; and thou shalt be a blessing.
>
> And I will bless them that bless thee, and curse him that curseth thee: and in thee shall all families of the earth be blessed. (Genesis 12:1-3)

God specifically prophesied that Abraham and his people would be faced with those who would curse them. In this generation, many nations are cursing Israel and...

I PREDICT: God is ready to judge all nations with hatred toward the seed of Abraham.

At least ten times God appeared to Abraham and promised him the land we know as Israel, Palestine, the Holy Land, or the Middle East.

The Old Testament, from the book of Genesis onward, maintains a consistent claim that God promised the patriarch Abraham the land over which he wandered and in which he lived. In that land this nation is to become the Divine instrument, to be a light to the nations and to declare God's salvation to the ends of the earth.

The New Testament takes up the promise and shows that it will become reality at the end of the age. Ezekiel's prophecy in chapters 38 and 39 refer to that fulfillment. The land promised to Abraham nearly four thousand years ago is *the land of promise and of prophecy*.

Although the contemporary state of Israel is a small country the size of Wales, the ancient nation of Israel occupied a larger area. God's promises to Abraham and his successors define a greater expanse of territory destined to form the Holy Land. Not only modern Israel, but a number of other sovereign states will eventually be merged to form the stage upon which this last act in the drama of prophecy will be enacted.

A significant expression in verse 12 of Ezekiel 38 declares the regathered nation dwells at the center of the earth. This is, geographically, literally true of the land of Israel. The circle of latitude that passes through the Middle East traverses the greatest length of land, nearly ten thousand miles from the China Sea to the Mediterranean Sea. Israel is situated at the junction of three continents: Europe, Asia, and Africa. It is roughly midway in distance between the west coast of Africa and the east coast of China. Also, it is midway between the southernmost border of Africa and the northernmost border of Siberia. If a point had to be selected which could be said to be the center of the land masses of the earth, Israel would logically be that point. More than anywhere else, it can claim to be called the center of the earth.

TITLE DEEDS

This is the land as it will be when Israel becomes the "holy nation" of the end time.

Ezekiel described this conflict in Ezekiel 35:5, "...thou hast had a perpetual hatred, and hast shed the blood of the children of Israel."

This hateful conflict is shown to be perpetual in past times by the words of Psalm 137:7, "Remember, O Lord, the children of Edom in the day of Jerusalem; who said, Rase it, rase it, even to the foundation thereof."

Scriptures show that it will continue, even though there may be periods of quiet, when the flames burn low, however, they will flare up again until the ...

> ...house of Jacob shall be a fire, and the house of Joseph a flame, and the house of Esau for stubble, and they shall kindle in them, and devour them; and there shall not be any remaining of the house of Esau; for the LORD hath spoken it.
> (Obadiah 18).

Of course, the Arabic people claim the land of Israel to be theirs. The Word of God, speaking prophetically, records this claim in Ezekiel 35:10:

> Because thou (Edom and the present day Arabs) hast said, These two nations and these two countries shall be mine, and we will possess it; whereas the LORD was there.

The meaning is that the present-day Arabs claim that the "two countries," Judah and Samaria, will be theirs and that they will "possess it." This is precisely the great issue.

That claim is further emphasized and expressed in Ezekiel 36:1-2, 5, (NIV)

> O mountains of Israel, hear the word of the
> LORD...The enemy said of you, "Aha! The an-
> cient heights have become our possession"...the
> nations...and...Edom.

The world knows this is the case today.

In modern times, certain events have intensified the Israeli-Arab conflict. The Zionist
Movement intensified it. This movement was
founded by Dr. Theodore Herzl in 1896. His
pamphlet The Jewish State stirred up great
interest in Zion and began the present modern
movement of Hebrews to the land of Israel. The
next year, 1897, the first Zionist Congress met
in Switzerland. The words of Ezekiel 37:21
were engraved on a medal struck to commem-
orate the National Federation of the Zionist
Movement.

> ...Behold, I will take the children of Israel from
> among the heathen, whither they be gone, and
> will gather them on every side, and bring them
> into their own land.

THE BALFOUR DECLARATION

World War I (1914-1918) also added fuel
to the Israeli-Arab conflict. The Turkish Empire joined forces with Germany, and the war
was carried to Palestine in October, 1914.

In 1916, Hebrew leaders met with British
Government leaders and discussed the creation

of an autonomous Jewish settlement in Palestine. On November 2, 1917, the famous Balfour Declaration was proclaimed pledging itself to:

(1) "the establishment in Palestine of a national home for the Jewish people.

(2) "it being clearly understood that nothing shall be done which may prejudice the civil and religious rights of existing non-Jewish communities in Palestine."

That declaration did not please the Arabs. They claimed that in 1914-1915 Great Britain promised to respect their sovereignty in Palestine. A dilemma was certainly created and Great Britain found herself in a perplexing predicament.

In 1922, the League of Nations gave the mandate over Palestine to Great Britain; and that, as it turned out, also intensified the Israeli-Arab conflict.

In 1937, the Israeli-Arab conflict had become so intense the British called it irrepressible. A commission decided on a division of the land. This was vigorously opposed by both parties. The land was divided into a Palestinian section and a Jewish section by the United Nations and the new State of Israel was born in 1948. Instantly, five Arab nations declared war on the newborn nation. Israel, with the same remarkable strength of little David against the giant Goliath, not only defended her right to exist, but also annexed additional territories. With seemingly miraculous vigor, Israel has withstood attacks and wars. The Arab drive to annihilate Israel forced the individual Arab states into a previously unheard of union in January of 1964 when the thirteen nations of Egypt, Sudan, Lebanon, Jordan, Syria, Iraq, Yemen, Libya, Tunisia, Algeria and Morocco met in Cairo to form the Arab Confederation. Never before had Arab nations been able to subdue their hatreds. They now united in a concerted move against Israel.

Israel has another enemy—the Soviet Union.

During two fateful days in June 1967, when Israel's military had devastated Arab armor, the Soviet Union came perilously close to war. Over the "hotline" from Moscow, the Russians were threatening to intercede in the Arab-Israeli conflict. America stood ready to stop them if they tried.

Why did the two superpowers risk a confrontation that might have brought nuclear disaster to the world? The answer lies in the character and content of the Middle East.

This strategic, tension-ridden area contains

60 percent of the world's oil reserves, and provides the shortest air and sea routes between Europe and southern Asia. For twenty years it has been a critical area in the cold war and a prime target of Soviet foreign policy.

MASKED SOVIET DESIGNS IN THE MIDDLE EAST

Despite the blunder of the Six-Day War—which cost the USSR $2 billion—the Kremlin has gone on to entrench and expand its power in this area. The countdown to a new and more ominous confrontation has already begun.

The Soviet Union's aggressive global war tactics in the Middle East—and the United States' policy of drift—could plunge the world into atomic proliferation against which the Kremlin has been piously preaching.

The minds of thinking men today are pondering the trend of the times and reaching conclusions which students of Bible prophecy have long held: the time of Jacob's (or Israel's) trouble is at hand. In this connection, we are forcibly reminded of our Lord's own words:

> Men's hearts failing them for fear, and for looking after those things which are coming on the earth... (Luke 21:26)

RUSSIA ATTEMPTS TO TITLE DEED THE LAND

After many days thou shalt be visited: in the latter years thou shalt come into the land that is brought back from the sword, and is gathered out of many people, against the mountains of Israel, which have been always waste: but it is brought forth out of the nations, and they shall dwell safely all of them.

Thou shalt ascend and come like a storm, thou shalt be like a cloud to cover the land, thou, and all thy bands, and many people with thee.

Thus saith the Lord GOD; It shall also come to pass, that at the same time shall things come into thy mind, and thou shalt think an evil thought:

And thou shalt say, I will go up to the land of unwalled villages; I will go to them that are at rest, that dwell safely, all of them dwelling without walls, and having neither bars nor gates,

To take a spoil, and to take a prey; to turn thine hand upon the desolate places that are now inhabited, and upon the people that are gathered out of the nations, which have gotten cattle and goods, that dwell in the midst of the land.

Ezekiel 38:8-12

The invasion of the Holy Land by the hosts of Russia (Gog and Magog) is one of the last great events of this age.

A clear understanding of the prophecy in the light both of Biblical and contemporary knowledge is an essential for those who desire to keep abreast with the unfolding of the Divine Plan.

Quite clearly, this passage is directly related to the Divine destiny of Israel in the end time and to the establishment of the Kingdom, and must therefore be understood in a dispensational sense and in an earthly setting. The time of the prophecy is the end of this age and the place of its fulfillment is upon this earth.

Russia will attack Israel in an attempt to control this geographically strategic position, capture the Mid-East oil reserves, and defy the God of Israel. However, the Bear will meet with a devastating defeat on the plains of Megiddo.

And it shall come to pass at the same time when Gog shall come against the land of Israel, saith the Lord GOD, that my fury shall come up in my face.

For in my jealousy and in the fire of my wrath have I spoken, Surely in that day there shall be a great shaking in the land of Israel;

So that the fishes of the sea, and the fowls of the heaven, and the beasts of the field, and all creeping things that creep upon the earth, and all the men that are upon the face of the earth, shall shake at my presence, and the mountains shall be thrown down, and the steep places shall fall, and every wall shall fall to the ground.

And I will call for a sword against him throughout all my mountains, saith the Lord GOD: every man's sword shall be against his brother.

And I will plead against him with pestilence and with blood; and I will rain upon him, and upon his bands, and upon the many people that are with him, an overflowing rain, and great hailstones, fire, and brimstone.

Thus will I magnify myself, and sanctify myself; and I will be known in the eyes of many nations, and they shall know that I am the LORD.

(Ezekiel 38:18-23)

Therefore, thou son of man, prophesy against Gog, and say, Thus saith the Lord GOD; Behold, I am against thee, O Gog, the chief prince of Meshech and Tubal:

And I will turn thee back, and leave but the sixth part of thee, and will cause thee to come up from the north parts, and will bring thee upon the mountains of Israel:

And I will smite thy bow out of thy left hand, and will cause thine arrows to fall out of thy right hand.

Thou shalt fall upon the mountains of Israel, thou, and all thy bands, and the people that is with thee: I will give thee unto the ravenous birds of every sort, and to the beasts of the field to be devoured.

Thou shalt fall upon the open field: for I have spoken it, saith the Lord GOD.

And I will send a fire on Magog, and among them that dwell carelessly in the isles: and they shall know that I am the LORD. (Ezekiel 39:1-6)

The decimation will be so complete that only one out of every six Red soldiers will return home.

This sets the final stage for the Common Market of Europe to become planet Earth's greatest potential power and from it will emerge the man of sin, the Antichrist, who will combat the God of Heaven.

6

I PREDICT:

THE COMMON MARKET OF EUROPE WILL RULE THE WORLD BEFORE 2000 A.D.

In the prophecy of Daniel the Prophet, chapter two, the enormous metallic giant represented the mighty empires of human history.

The last of the vast empires is the Roman Empire. It was first divided by the legs of the giant, representing the Eastern and Western powers. Their seats of authority were Constantinople in Asia and Rome in Europe.

The final expression of this empire is in the feet—the ten toes. This speaks of ten end-time kingdoms of the last days.

The man Daniel, through supernatural power, saw the entire scope of all world empires.

The vision had to do only with those empires prophetically involved with world destiny.

The vision of a statue with a head of gold, shoulders and breast of silver, thighs of brass and legs of iron is not man's conception of empires. It is God's conception.

King Nebuchadnezzar's vision gave the imposing outward glory of the destiny of empires. God revealed their natures in Daniel, chapter 7. It is an important contrast.

THE PAGAN KING SEES A VISION

In Daniel 2, God revealed through Daniel that the great metallic colossus foretold the future of mankind in governments.

The metallic man revealed four great, prophetic world empires. These cover the entire period of Gentile supremacy in the world.

1) A Unit Head: Babylon is represented by the head of gold.

Daniel 2:38 says, "...Thou art this head of gold."

2) Dual 2: The Medo-Persian Empire is represented by silver. Daniel 2:39 says it is inferior to the first empire. It represents the arms and chest of the metallic wonder.

3) Quadruple 4: The Grecian Empire began as a monarchy under Alexander, but was later controlled by four army generals. It is represented by brass.

4) End 10 Toes: The Roman Empire is represented by iron and clay. The final world rulership is represented by the iron and clay of the feet of the image. This speaks of the strength of dictatorship and the weakness of democracy in the end time.

UNDERSTANDING EMPIRES

The interpretation of Nebuchadnezzar's dream teaches us several things about the history of the world from that date to the end of the present age.

It teaches that God, having removed Israel as a political factor, has in the meantime committed all power and dominion of the earth into the hands of Gentile nations.

BABYLONIAN EMPIRE
Thou art the head of Gold
(Daniel 2:38)

Lion
Daniel 7:4

Gold

B.C. 538

68 YEARS

MEDO-PERSIAN EMPIRE
*After thee shall arise another
kingdom inferior to thee*
(Daniel 2:39)

Bear
Daniel 7:5

Silver

B.C. 331

207 YEARS

GRECIAN EMPIRE
*Another third kingdom of
brass which shall bear
rule over all the earth*
(Daniel 2:39b)

Leopard
Daniel 7:6

Brass

B.C. 146

185 YEARS

ROMAN EMPIRE
*And the fourth kingdom
shall be strong as iron*
(Daniel 2:40)

DIVISION OF EMPIRE
A.D. 395

Iron

Strange Beast
Daniel 7:8,9

Iron & Clay
Teeth of Iron - Rule
Ten Horns - Kings
Little Horn - Antichrist

AD 364 TO COMING OF CHRIST

THE TIMES OF THE GENTILES APPROXIMATELY 2500 YEARS

Eastern World of Rome
British Rule at Jerusalem

Western World of Rome
American Power at Jerusalem

TEN KINGDOMS OF ANTICHRIST   COMMUNISM AND DEMOCRACY

THE COURSE AND END OF THE GENTILE WORLD SYSTEM IS GIVEN BY DANIEL

The four metals composing the enormous image are explained as symbolizing four empires, fulfilled in Babylon, Medo-Persia, Greece and Rome. The latter power is seen divided first into two (the legs), fulfilled in the Eastern and Western Roman empires, and then into ten kingdoms (the toes). The toes represent the federation of nations—under one head, the Antichrist—which will exist at the end of the present age.

THE STONE OF DESTINY

The smiting stone (Daniel 2:34-35) destroys the Gentile world system by a sudden and irremediable blow. It is not by the gradual process of conversion and assimilation. Then, and not before, does the stone become a mountain which fills the whole earth. The detail of the end time is given in Daniel chapter 7, and Revelation chapters 13 through 19. It is important to see that Gentile world power is to end in sudden catastrophic judgment; the battle of Armageddon. It is noteworthy that Gentile world dominion begins and ends with a huge image (Daniel 2:21, Revelation 13:14-15).

We are nearing the end of the times of the Gentiles; evidence of this is on every hand. Israel was reborn as a national entity, a world government is in formation, a world church is in formation and worldwide moral deterioration is rampant.

Notice the devolution of human government from gold to clay. The specific gravity, or weight of gold, is 19.5; of silver, 10.47; of brass, 8.0; of cast iron, 5.0; of clay, 1.93. There is also a diminishing value from substance to substance.

This colossus of human government becomes top heavy from gold to mud. Its crumbling feet depict the hour in which we live today.

EMPIRES WITHOUT GOD

Man has eternally attempted to set up a kingdom without God. This began with Nimrod who built Babylon. It was continued with Assyria, Egypt, Persia, Greece, and Rome.

Man has made six successive attempts and failures to establish world empires without God.

We are nearing the greatest change in human history when Christ shall come and set up His Kingdom and the total of all empires shall fall into the dust heap of history.

Forasmuch as thou sawest that the stone was cut out of the mountain without hands, and that it brake in pieces the iron, the brass, the clay, the silver, and the gold; the great God hath made known to the king what shall come to pass hereafter: and the dream is certain, and the interpretation thereof sure. (Daniel 2:45)

THE HUMANIST WORLD DICTATOR SHALL RULE BEFORE 2000 A.D.

I predict that a world leader of unprecedented proportions will soon emerge. He will bring unusual peace and prosperity to the earth for a short season.

Following these "golden years," he will throw the world into the greatest turmoil ever. This great world leader will not appear from the expected political circles of Russia or the United States. In fact, as we have just learned, the Communist Bloc will be suddenly divested of its place of world prominence. This post-Gog leader will arise from the sea of humanity with political power over ten European nations which are historically rooted in the Roman Empire. A miraculous recovery from an assassination attempt will propel him to the forefront of the news media and into the minds and hearts of the universal human race. His spiritual companion will continually astound the nations and convince them that this political-spiritual duo is divinely destined for world rulership.

The Bible records the rise to power of this end time superstar in Revelation 13:1-6:

> And I stood upon the sand of the sea, and saw a beast rise up out of the sea, having seven heads and ten horns, and upon his horns ten crowns, and upon his heads the name of blasphemy.
>
> And the beast which I saw was like unto a leopard, and his feet were as the feet of a bear, and his mouth as the mouth of a lion: and the dragon gave him his power, and his seat, and great authority.
>
> And I saw one of his heads as it were wounded to death; and his deadly wound was healed: and all the world wondered after the beast.
>
> And they worshipped the dragon which gave power unto the beast: and they worshipped the beast, saying, Who is like unto the beast? who is able to make war with him?
>
> And there was given unto him a mouth speaking great things and blasphemies; and power was given unto him to continue forty and two months.
>
> And he opened his mouth in blasphemy against God, to blaspheme his name, and his tabernacle, and them that dwell in heaven.

ANTICHRIST RELIGION

> And I beheld another beast coming up out of the earth; and he had two horns like a lamb, and he spake as a dragon.

And he exerciseth all the power of the first beast before him, and causeth the earth and them which dwell therein to worship the first beast, whose deadly wound was healed.

And he doeth great wonders, so that he maketh fire come down from heaven on the earth in the sight of men,

And he deceiveth them that dwell on the earth by the means of those miracles which he had power to do in the sight of the beast; saying to them that dwell on the earth, that they should make an image to the beast, which had the wound by a sword, and did live.

And he had power to give life unto the image of the beast, that the image of the beast should both speak, and cause that as many as would not worship the image of the beast should be killed.

And he causeth all, both small and great, rich and poor, free and bond, to receive a mark in their right hand, or in their foreheads:

And that no man might buy or sell, save he that had the mark, or the name of the beast, or the number of his name.

Here is wisdom. Let him that hath understanding count the number of the beast: for it is the number of a man; and his number is Six hundred threescore and six. (Revelation 13:11-18)

This mystery man of the 666 will appear only after a period of apostasy in the nominal churches. Unconcern for the things of God in the church is an open invitation for the devil to take control.

Now we beseech you, brethren, by the coming of our Lord Jesus Christ, and by our gathering together unto him.

That ye be not soon shaken in mind, or be troubled, neither by spirit, not by word, nor by letter as from us, as that the day of Christ is at hand.

Let no man deceive you by any means: for that day shall not come, except there come a falling away first, and *that man of sin be revealed, the son of perdition.*

Who opposeth and exalteth himself above all that is called God, or that is worshipped; so that he as God sitteth in the temple of God, shewing himself that he is God. (II Thessalonians 2:1-4)

The wonder ruler will move his regal seat from Europe to the glorious land of Israel. The move will signify the beginning of a reign of terror rather than the utopian society he had promised.

He shall enter also into the glorious land, and many countries shall be overthrown: but these shall escape out of his hand, even Edom, and Moab, and the chief of the children of Ammon.
(Daniel 11:41)

Behold, the day of the Lord cometh, and thy spoil shall be divided in the midst of thee.

For I will gather all nations against Jerusalem to battle; and the city shall be taken, and the houses rifled, and the women ravished; and half of the city shall go forth into captivity, and the residue of the people shall not be cut off from the city.
(Zechariah 14:1-2)

And it shall come to pass, that in all the land, saith
the LORD, two parts therein shall be cut off and
die; but the third shall be left therein.

And I will bring the third part through the fire, and
will refine them as silver is refined, and will try
them as gold is tried: they shall call on my name,
and I will hear them: I will say, It is my people:
and they shall say, The LORD is my God.
(Zechariah 13:8-9)

Antichrist's authority will soon prove to be
demonic and will become apparent that his purpose is to bring a physical and spiritual conflict with the nation of Israel and good people
everywhere. John the Revelator saw this conflict
in visionary form as a red dragon trying to
devour a woman clothed in the sun. Israel and
the manchild to which she gave birth (the
Church) are the prey of the Antichrist ruler.
However, God will prepare a way of escape
during the bloody reign of the Great Tribulation.

And there appeared a great wonder in heaven; a
woman clothed with the sun, and the moon under
her feet, and upon her head a crown of twelve
stars:

And she being with child cried, travailing in birth,
and pained to be delivered.

And there appeared another wonder in heaven;
and behold a great red dragon, having seven
heads and ten horns, and seven crowns upon his
heads.

And his tail drew the third part of the stars of
heaven, and did cast them to the earth: and the
dragon stood before the woman which was ready
to be delivered, for to devour her child as soon
as it was born.

And she brought forth a man child, who was to
rule all nations with a rod of iron: and her child
was caught up unto God, and to his throne.

And the woman fled into the wilderness, where
she hath a place prepared of God, that they should
feed her there a thousand two hundred and
threescore days. (Revelation 12:1-6)

Finally the great champion of all ages—the
victorious resurrected General of Heaven—will
appear to destroy the Antichrist and to put a
final end to evil.

And I saw heaven opened, and behold a white
horse; and he that sat upon him was called Faithful
and True, and in righteousness he doth judge and
make war. (Revelation 19:11)

Antichrist will gather the nations to Jerusalem
to fight against God. However, he will find that
he has met his final Waterloo. The humanist
world dictator will fall at the feet of the Divine
Universal King.

In consummation of human history, Christ
will reign for one thousand years. He will
obliterate the seven years of humanistic rule
with one thousand years of peace.

I PREDICT A WORLDWIDE SPIRITUAL REVOLUTION BEFORE 2000 A.D.

But there is the other side of the future: the ebb and the flow.

When we say that a mighty revival is going to flow, it is similar to a rising tide or a boisterous wave.

It is exciting if you live near Waikiki beach. Each wave wears a crested crown of sparkling white as it pushes forward in a beautiful curl toward the sable sands.

The ebb, your dictionary says, is the "return of the wave." After breaking upon the sands, it begins a recession into the sea. The water recedes. The waves recede.

The ebb is movement of the water on the bottom, not on the top. The wave being sucked underneath is called an undertow.

Spiritually speaking, I prophesy a wave of spiritual revolution and simultaneously, an ebb.

You can live in the flow of God, the incoming wave. It is the wave of the future! Whatever God is going to do tomorrow, you can be ready for it.

It is true there have been false situations where religious groups rose up and said, "We are the wave of the future." When they are not of God the ebb (the undertow) comes, and they are gone. You no longer see them on the face of the earth.

METHODIST WAVE

My mother witnessed the mighty wave of Wesleyanism and Methodism in America. She had three uncles who were circuit riders or Methodist rural preachers. They traveled mostly by horseback. They loved God. They prayed. They sought the Lord. They preached the Word out of the Bible. They never said, "The Bible says this and means something else." They said, "The Bible says what it means, and means what it says."

However, in my day, I have lived to see the ebb of this revival. It is receding back the other way; the membership is getting smaller and smaller. There is little revival and few who are getting people saved.

We must decide whether we want to be in the *wave of God* or in the *ebb of religion*.

SALVATION ARMY WAVE

I saw the Salvation Army in this wave of

the future. I preached for the Salvation Army in Dublin, Ireland, when they were the largest evangelical group in the Irish Republic. On a Sunday night, they had 1500 people. I was amazed that they were so strong for winning souls. In England, the Salvation Army were soulwinners. They would go to the corner and preach and sing and get sinners saved and take them back to their chapel to teach them. Then slowly they became a church of feeding and clothing people. Now many think that all they ever did is just give people food and clothes. Of course, that is good, but do not forget they were born as one of the mightiest revivals in the history of mankind. Their first leaders often went to jail, not for handing out food, but for preaching the gospel of Jesus on the street corners of London.

In religious revivals very often there is a flow and there is an ebb. I believe, at the same time there is an ebb in one place, there is a flow in another! People must choose whether they want to be in the undercurrent or the uppercurrent during their lifetime.

In Joel 2:28, God predicts that in the last days He will pour out of His spirit upon all flesh. If there were enough of the pouring out of God's Spirit in Russia, the United States would not have to spend billions of dollars in armaments.

The Spirit of God would make the difference. The wave of the future is for all of us. God loves all of us. There is nobody little and nobody big. We are all beautiful in God's sight.

The wave of the future has a relationship with the ministering of angels. More and more of us will know the ministry of angels. It is going to be exciting.

The wave of the future is going to be a church full of love.

In Jeremiah 33:9, God said that what the Church does will be...

> ...to me a name of joy, a praise and an honour before all the nations of the earth, which shall hear all the good that I do unto them: and they shall fear and tremble for all the goodness and for all the prosperity that I procure unto it.

You have to be prosperous before you can make the church prosperous. There is only one enemy to the wave of the future and that is unbelief and sin. You have to get those things out and then you can have the wave of God's future flowing. I do not want to be with the ebbing tide. I want to be with the wave of the future. That is what God wants us to be. He is ready to bless us.

THE WAVE OF THE FUTURE IS COMING!

And it shall come to pass afterward, that I will pour
out my spirit upon all flesh; and your sons and
your daughters shall prophesy, your old men shall
dream dreams, your young men shall see visions.
(Joel 2:28)

The gifts of the Spirit will flow.

There will be miracles of healing for millions
of people.

The wave of the future will be a ministry of
angels for the Body of Christ.

It will be a church of love and zeal.

Get ready! The wave of the future is on its
way!

That is the best way to beat the demonic
antichrist system.

7

I PREDICT:

TIME WILL RUN OUT
BY 2000 A.D.

Man experiences three main limitations while living on planet Earth. He is limited by *time*. It cuts man short of his ambitions.

Secondly, man is limited by *space*. He can only be in one place at a time.

The third is *energy*. All energy of man is calibrated and limited.

The fateful year of 2000 A.D. is approaching. Leaders have a foreboding that important changes on planet Earth are about to happen. The Kiplinger Letter, written and mailed in the mid-eighties, already warned man to prepare for 2000 A.D.

TIME IS A MYSTERY

All humans are given a limited piece of time. Nobody can get along without it, yet everybody has difficulty explaining it. We talk about work time, leisure time, day time, good times, bad times, old times. No one has been able to clearly define time. One philosopher said, "Time is a form of thought under which we relate events to each other and to ourselves." Time is a measure of motion. Time is a duration of energy.

TIME IS RELATIVITY

Our world is caught up in time. We speak about the swift industrialization of Africa, bringing change in a short period of time.

We talk about telescoping time, or having time stand still. For a boy, an hour in his school book and an hour on the ball field are two different time limits. Time actually crawls for a prisoner in jail. To youth under a romantic moon, time flies. The watch is the same gauge, but emotion makes it different.

TIME IS PRECIOUS

Time is precious because once experienced

it cannot be recalled. We receive a bill from a repairman and find that although the part costs 50¢, we are charged $10 to put it in. Time is more precious than material.

When time is running out, men will give everything in the world for it. One millionaire screamed at his death, "I would give a million dollars for one more hour to live."

TIME IS OPPORTUNITY

A Greek word for time is *chronos.* It means duration, but its meaning has nothing to do with quality or character. From this word we get our word "chronometer," or a time piece.

The Greeks have another word for time, *kairos,* which means meaningful time, or critical times. This is the word used in Ephesians 5:16 when it says, "redeeming the time, because the days are evil."

There are plenty of "chronometers" or time pieces in our world, but we need "kairometers" or devices telling us how critical or opportune a time situation is. With a seeing eye and an open mind, meaningful achievement is accomplished.

TIME IS EQUALITY

Time has no favorites. It is impartial. It gives each person 60 seconds per minute, 60 minutes per hour, and 8,670 hours per year. Everyone has the same amount of time per day. It is the management of time and not its measure that makes the difference.

TIME IS URGENCY

Jesus said in John 9:4, "I must work the works of him that sent me while it is day, the night cometh when no man can work."

Jesus Christ was caught up in the wheels of time for just over thirty and three years.

The great missionary Robert Moffet said, "We have all eternity to celebrate our victories, we have but one short hour before sunset to win them."

Our world has urgent needs and time is running out. We must become more conscious of time.

The Preacher in Ecclesiastes 3:1,11 observes...

To every thing there is a *season,* and a *time* to every purpose under the heaven.

He hath made every thing beautiful *in his time:*

also he hath set the world in their heart, so that
no man can find out the work that God maketh
from the beginning to the end.

TIME IS PROPHETIC

Looking at the past, dramatic events have
taken place in the earth at the changing of
significant millennia.

For example, 2000 years after Adam the
world suffered the catastrophic flood, and
only Noah and his family of eight survived to
tell the story.

At the calendar year 4000 after Adam, the
world Savior was born. "But when the fulness
of the time was come, God sent forth his
Son..." (Galatians 4:4). The whole of human
history changed directions.

At the 6000th year, Christ is to return and
establish His Kingdom on planet Earth. To the
world this is terrifying.

In the first 2000 years of man's history,
Christ was manifested as *the Prophet.*

In the second 2000 years of man's history,
Christ was manifested as *the Priest.*

In the final 1000 years Christ is manifested

as *the King.* In eternity Christ is manifested as all three simultaneously!

At the termination of the first 2000 years, planet Earth experienced its first rain, its first thunder and lightning. The earth changed.

At the end of the second time period of 2000 years, the earth quaked, the great veil of the temple was torn asunder and terminated Jewish temple worship. The world was never the same again.

At the end of the third period of 2000 years, there shall be wars, famines, earthquakes and plagues before the establishing of the eternal Kingdom of David in Jerusalem where Jesus Christ shall reign.

Also, the first 2000 years up to Noah's day can represent the functions of the Father God.

The second 2000 years ending at Calvary represent the administration of the Son.

The third 2000 years, which are man in the wind down of terminations, reveal the ministry of the Holy Ghost.

I predict the absolute fullness of man's operation on planet Earth by the year 2000 A.D. Then Jesus Christ shall reign from Jerusalem for 1000 years.

RACING TOWARD 2000 A.D.

Planet Earth is racing against the clock! The clock is ticking off hours and minutes. That clock says the midnight hour approaches like a time bomb. Those who look for Christ's coming must run with the news. **The Church has the key to the future.** Our world trembles before the mystic year of 2000 A.D. when there is not only a change of centuries, but also a change of millennia. Could this be the end of time?

> And I saw another mighty angel come down from heaven, clothed with a cloud: and a rainbow was upon his head, and his face was as it were the sun, and his feet as pillars of fire:
>
> And the angel which I saw stand upon the sea and upon the earth lifted up his hand to heaven,
>
> And sware by him that liveth for ever and ever, who created heaven, and the things that therein are, and the earth, and the things that therein are, and the sea, and the things which are therein, that there should be time no longer. (Rev. 10:1,5-6)

Great mysteries and wonders await this year's second graders by 2000 A.D. Prophecy will have been fulfilled. science will have progressed beyond today's boundaries of knowledge. Our houses will be different to live in. The morality of the home will be different. The general morality of nations will be different. Today's television child will then be ruling society. The general mentality of world leaders will be different. They will have experienced world government. Independence will be at the lowest ebb of human history.

I predict the currency that will be used as money will be different. It will be a global coinage. There will be universal money.

New forces will shape the globe in 2000 A.D. Are you ready for the change which is advancing with amazing speed?

Today, a child born in America is shackled by his part of the National Debt, which is about $8,000.00. This means the new citizens of America are born in debt and even by 2000 A.D. will not be out!

When the bells ring out to welcome the year 2000 A.D....

- The international police will keep the peace.
- The world economy will be controlled by a committee of foreigners.
- The Government is making the laws for One World that is strongly controlled by "Big Brother" of George Orwell's 1984 A.D.

WILL YOU BE READY FOR DESTINY?

8

I PREDICT:

JERUSALEM WILL BECOME THE GREATEST AND RICHEST CITY ON PLANET EARTH BEFORE 2000 A.D.

I predict that Jerusalem, more than ever before in history, will be the focal point of world action. From today to the year 2000 A.D. there is a count down for Jerusalem.

The unique capital city of Israel linking the Middle East—part of the continent of Asia—to Africa and Europe, is the hub of the intercontinental wheel, whose spokes lead to the ruling cities of history.

Jerusalem is the birthplace and heartthrob

of all the great monotheistic religions of the world. It has more religious zeal than any other city on planet Earth. This birthplace of religions, however, has also been the burial place of empires.

The Babylonian Empire died on the night that its king stooped to the grossest mockery of God.

Similarly, in modern times I believe the demise of the British Empire began in this century with its mistreatment of the Jews and its mishandling of Palestine, starting at the end of World War I.

When I began my ministry in the 1930s and shortly therafter toured the world with Howard Carter of London, England, Great Britain was still the major global empire. Without doubt, Britannia still ruled the waves. It controlled nations all over the earth. But its decline began when its Parliament favored the Arabs over Israel. By 1948, when British forces left Palestine, England's empire was waning.

Please hear me. The same fate of fading awaits America if its support of Israel does not remain strong.

Psalm 46:5 says of Jerusalem, "God is in the midst of her; she shall not be moved: God shall help her, just at the break of dawn.."

In Zechariah 1:14 God said, "I am zealous for Jerusalem and for Zion with great zeal."

In Psalm 129:5 we read, "Let all those who hate Zion be put to shame and turned back."

In contrast to that, the inspired writer of Psalm 122:6 said of Jerusalem, "Pray for the peace of Jerusalem: they shall prosper that love thee."

The message is clear: despite the many failings of the Israeli people in their city of Jerusalem, God has chosen them and determined to bless them. Accordingly, He will also bless those who bless Jerusalem, but He will bring low those who harm the seed of Abraham.

Spreading over the entire Middle East and North Africa are constant threatenings of war. They center in Jerusalem, Israel. These nations have deep controversy with Israel and Jerusalem.

They all say, "Who will master Jerusalem in 2000 A.D.?"

It is strange, but the first letter of some of the nations surrounding Israel spell "Israel."

I   IRAQ (North and east of Jerusalem)

S   SYRIA (North and east of Jerusalem)

R   ROYAL HASHMITE KINGDOM OF JORDAN (East of Jerusalem)

A   ARABIA SAUDIA (South and east of Jerusalem)

E   EGYPT (West and south of Jerusalem)

L   LEBANON (North of Jerusalem)

THE MESSIAH RETURNS TO JERUSALEM

The world empires die at Jerusalem. Her plains north of her are in Megiddo. The writer of Revelation indicates with exactness that Megiddo is the geographical location of the last battlefield of the present age, a struggle that will eclipse anything that history has ever known.

Armageddon will be the finale of the age-long struggle which began in Eden. So powerfully has the concept of Armageddon entered into the thinking of man that the Oxford English Dictionary actually defines the word "Armageddon" as "the place of the last decisive battle at the day of judgment: hence used illustratively for any final conflict on a great scale."

Antichrist will make a covenant with the Jews in the early part of the national resurrection. He will break this agreement. The covenant with Israel will be the final issue of the Antichrist's reign.

The armies of the Antichrist and the kings of the earth under his leadership will be gathered in Megiddo to war against the Jews and their Messiah.

The Antichrist will be the general of the earthly forces.

And I saw the beast, and the kings of the earth, and their armies, gathered together to make war against him that sat on the horse, and against his army. (Revelation 19:19)

The Lord Jesus Christ will be the general of the Heavenly Armies.

And I saw heaven opened, and behold a white horse; and he that sat upon him was called Faithful and True, and in righteousness he doth judge and make war. (Revelation 19:11)

This last great battle of the ages will come at the end of the Great Tribulation. Jesus, the Son of God, will bring the battle to a successful conclusion.

And the remnant were slain with the sword of him that sat upon the horse, which sword proceeded

out of his mouth: and all the fowls were filled with
their flesh. (Revelation 19:21)

When the devil is completely defeated, planet
Earth will enter into a new age, the Millennium.
At that time Jesus will rule the earth.

And I saw an angel come down from heaven, having the key of the bottomless pit and a great chain
in his hand.

And he laid hold on the dragon, that old serpent,
which is the Devil, and Satan, and bound him a
thousand years. (Revelation 20:1-2)

JERUSALEM, CITY OF SORROW

Jerusalem is the most invaded city of human
history. Nearly every world empire at one time
has conquered or dominated the capital of
Israel. The history of mankind can be written
in Jerusalem's blood.

The political situation in Jerusalem always
indicated its spiritual condition. When Israel had
apostasy in the soul, there was political slavery.
When revival came to the temple, there was
prosperity on the throne.

There remains until A.D. 2000 woeful controversy against Jerusalem and Israel. God said,

Behold, I will make Jerusalem a cup of trembling
unto all the people round about, when they shall
be in the siege both against Judah and against
Jerusalem.

And in that day will I make Jerusalem a burden-
some stone for all people: all that burden
themselves with it shall be cut in pieces, though
all the people of the earth be gathered together
against it. (Zechariah 12:2-3)

The Jews have never left Jerusalem volun-
tarily, but have always been led away as cap-
tives.

And they shall fall by the edge of the sword, and
shall be led away captive into all nations: and
Jerusalem shall be trodden down of the Gentiles,
until the times of the Gentiles be fulfilled.
(Luke 21:24)

Jesus was in the grave for two days and the
third day was the resurrection. The Jews were
dispersed among the nations for two days, or
two thousand years; on the third day they have
been regathered to Jerusalem. It is their resurrection time. Through the word of prophecy
they knew that one day they would return home
again.

We have also a more sure word of prophecy;
whereunto ye do well that ye take heed, as unto
a light that shineth in a dark place, until the day
dawn, and the day star arise in your hearts.
(II Peter 1:19)

I PREDICT JERUSALEM
TO BECOME RICH

Moscow, the capital of the Union of Soviet

Socialist Republic, is the communist mecca. The USSR is larger than all South America and more than twice the size of the United States of America. The land measures 5000 miles across.

Moscow is destined to send its confederates against Jerusalem and Israel.

When the time of Moscow's invasion of Israel comes, Ezekiel 38:10 says she "will make an evil plan." Perhaps the Russians will be after the great mineral wealth, including the oil, of the Middle East. Or maybe their goal will be to control Israel as the vital land bridge between three continents. Whatever their reasoning, behind it will be the counsel and prompting of Satan, who has always hated and sought to destroy God's chosen people, Israel, and has hated Jerusalem, the city God loves. The Bible describes the invasion this way:

> Then you will come from your place out of the far north, you and many peoples with you, all of them riding on horses, a great company and a mighty army.
>
> You will come up against My people Israel like a cloud, to cover the land. It will be in the latter days that I will bring you against My land. (Ezekiel 38:15-16 NIV)

WORLD COMMUNISM

Moscow's doom was written 2570 years ago. Behind closed doors plans have been carefully made by the wicked leaders of the USSR to annihilate Israel. In the past they have murdered millions from the Baltic Sea to the China Sea to achieve their goals. They will come out of the north like a storm and cover the land like a cloud. God's wrath will be aroused as they come against a land at rest. God said,

> My fury will show in My face. For in My jealousy and in the fire of My wrath I have spoken: 'Surely in that day there will be a great earthquake in the land of Israel.' (Ezekiel 38:18-19 NIV)

Russia's arrogance in attacking God's land and people will kindle God's anger and He will come to Israel's defense.

In verse 21 (NIV), God tells us,

> I will call for a sword against Gog (Russia) throughout all My mountains...Every man's sword will be against his brother.

Just what that means we cannot know for sure, but it may be that God will cause great confusion on the battlefield, with the Russians killing each other.

God further spoke by Ezekiel 38:22 (NIV),

I will rain down on him, on his troops, and on the many peoples who are with him, flooding rain, great hailstones, fire, and brimstone.

There will be a great flood that will bog down all Russian arrangements on the plain. Such a thing is not hard to imagine happening there, because the plain was actually a swamp until the early 1920s, when it was drained in a land reclamation project. This time, however, the water will come from a torrential downpour from the hand of God.

There will also be a pestilence of some kind that causes bleeding—very possibly dysentery. There will be fire and brimstone such as God used to destroy Sodom and Gomorrah in the time of Abraham.

What will be the result of this supernatural attack against the Russian invaders?

I (God) will turn you (Russia) around and lead you on...and bring you against the mountains of Israel,...I will give you to birds of prey of every sort and to the beasts of the field to be devoured.
(Ezekiel 29:2,4 NIV)

What destruction! The birds and other animals will eat the flesh off the dead bodies of the enemy.

We should note also that this defense of Israel will all be an act of God. The Jews will not lift a finger on this occasion until the conflict is over;

and thus all the glory will go to God, as He says in Ezekiel:

> Thus I will magnify Myself and sanctify Myself; and I will be known in the eyes of many nations, and they shall know that I am the LORD.

> So I will make My holy name known in the midst of My people Israel; and I will not let them profane My holy name any more: and the heathen shall know that I am the LORD, the Holy One in Israel. (Ezekiel 38:23; 39:7 NIV)

Moscow will meet its waterloo on the banks of the Jordan, the Sea of Galilee, the Suez Canal and the Mediterranean Sea. The USSR will no longer be a world conqueror, nor will it be a threat to Jerusalem and Israel.

Jerusalem by war will take all the riches of Moscow and its allies, including the Arab States. Jerusalem suddenly becomes the richest city on planet Earth.

The world government of the Antichrist will move his government there. The world will be gazing at the mystery of the new World Capitol City.

9

I PREDICT:

THE SEVEN PROPHECIES GOD GAVE ME SHALL BE FULFILLED BEFORE 2000 A.D.

These are possibly the most important words I have spoken to the United States of America.

Please hear me.

This prophecy began in Manila, Philippines. I had been invited by the President of the Philippines to a special meeting where he addressed local and foreign dignitaries in a joint congress. On one side of me was the Ambassador from the United States, on the other side a Roman Catholic archbishop.

After the meeting I walked out of the congress building and saw a public demonstration. Most of the harangue was against America rather than related to the Philippines. Signs being jogged up and down by young teenagers said, "Go home, white monkeys!" Others said, "America is imperialist!"

I walked out among the people and spoke to a boy who had a sign saying, "Go home, white monkey."

I said, "Son, am I a white monkey?"

He said, "No, Sir."

I said, "Well, that is what the sign says."

He replied, "Yes, Sir."

"Why are you carrying it?" I demanded.

He said, "I was given a few pesos to carry it."

"You really should throw that sign down. You may get hurt."

He threw it down and I stomped it to pieces to where no one could pick it up.

I walked over to the boy carrying the sign

"America is imperialist" and said, "Son, are you a student of history?"

He said, "No, Sir."

"Why are you carrying that sign?" I demanded.

He replied, "I was on the street over there and they gave me some pesos to carry it.

I said, "This is the way riots begin. Do you know anything about America?"

"No, Sir."

I said, "My country gave your country freedom twice. Our young men died in two wars in order to make your country free. They fought the Spaniards to set your people free and they fought the Japanese."

He admitted, "Yes, I have heard of that."

I continued, "We are not imperialists, are we?"

"No, Sir."

I said, "Then throw the sign down!"

He threw it down and I stomped it to pieces.

I love America and by this time tears were running down my face. I was ashamed to be in the crowd so I walked two blocks from the government buildings to our church.

I sat at my desk weeping, telling God how much I loved America and hated for it to be hurt by people who did not understand us. God spoke into my spirit and said, "Son, I am sending you home to live. You can go overseas to minister, but your headquarters will be in America." I could not quite understand that because my family and I were living in Manila. This was our second time to pastor the church there.

"Why, Lord?" I cried.

The Lord replied, "I am going to give you seven reasons why I am sending you home."

I took my pen and began to write down the reasons why I was to live in America.

HELP SAVE AMERICA

The Lord said, "I want you to help save America."

I replied, "Lord, I am willing to."

He said, "It is my bastion of freedom in the great world of the mind. The freedom to think in America can spread throughout the world. I need you to help save the freedom of minds."

"Lord, I am willing to be anything for you."

Then He spoke to me and said, "Through television I will give you *a million souls.*"

I was excited. "Lord, I will do anything for a million souls."

The Lord told me, "I will give you a million souls through television if you will go home. These are the seven things you will witness in America."

1) AMERICA TO DEPART FROM HISTORIC FAITH

"The first sign to observe is that America will depart from *the faith.* Like Israel America will depart from the faith of its fathers'. It will depart from historic truths and from fundamental preaching. It will forsake its original beliefs."

I cried out, "Lord, tell me about that."

The Lord said, "My Word prophetically declares in I Timothy 4:1, 'Now the Spirit speaketh expressly, that in the latter times some shall depart from the faith...' "

The Holy Spirit prophesies that many shall depart from the traditional faith. They shall depart from the Bible. They shall depart from the religion of their parents. They shall go out from truth.

I sat there saying to myself, "You cannot get *out* of a car until you get *into* a car. You cannot go *out* of a house until you get *into* a house. That means multitudes are going to walk out on their faith and abandon it!"

I became very hurt inside. God said, "You will see it. Millions will not go to church and not serve Me. They will just leave their faith."

2) AMERICA TO ENDORSE PAGAN RELIGIONS

While I paused for a moment, the Spirit of the Lord spoke forcibly to me saying, "Not only will millions depart from their faith, but Eastern religions which you have dealt with for many years and pagan religions, will take root in America and will flourish."

The Holy Spirit said that America would believe in strange gods. I Timothy 4:1 continues, "...giving heed to seducing spirits, and doctrines of devils."

The Lord said, "They will do it."

Pagan religions will become a prominent part of American life. Hinduism, with its 330 million demon gods, would invade America. We have seen this come to pass.

Thousands of people have taken up yoga. Yoga means to submit your mind to an unseen force while chanting words, called mantra, in the Hindu language that you do not understand. You are praising and praying to a Hindu god and you open your mind for demon power to enter that you might be possessed by the devil.

Hinduism is growing in this country in many forms. The Hare Krishnas, mostly led by young Americans, are showing that Hinduism can grow, and they come with a lie saying, "We are full of love!" But love is not their language. They picked up those words from Christianity. What they are doing is seducing people to leave and abandon their faith in the great and mighty God, who created the heavens and the earth, to accept a pagan religion with no hope in this life or in the life to come.

Doctrines of the Devil

As I thought on this, the Lord said, "Millions will depart from the faith, and give heed to or accept doctrines of the devil."

"That means demons telling lies, seducing men and women, like Eve was seduced in the Garden of Eden into taking of the fruit of the Tree of Knowledge of Good and Evil, bringing havoc upon the human race."

The devil's doctrines are:

A. Don't believe Jesus Christ is the Savior of the world.
B. Don't believe Jesus Christ's blood can cleanse from sin.
C. Don't believe Jesus Christ is coming again to receive us unto Himself.

Doctrines of devils always mean the opposite of doctrines of truth and life.

Sitting in my church in Manila, I could not believe what I was hearing.

Yet, I am seeing it. You, too, are seeing it today.

3) SATAN WORSHIP

The Lord continued, "Besides Oriental religions and cults of demon worship, satanic orgies will become prominent in America."

I replied, "Lord, how could that be in a nation built on the Bible? Our forefathers departed Europe where Satan worship was prominent. How could we go back into satanic worship?"

The Lord said, "They will go to fetishes and carry holy objects around and have covens where blood sacrifices are made."

You cannot imagine how affected I was. Having grown up in a society of evangelicalism, hearing the Lord tell me that our country would go backwards into idol worship, worshiping fetishes, worshiping satanic entities often related to human sacrifice. In witch covens in this country the government has discovered baby bones where human sacrifices to demon gods have been made.

On special assignment

I told the Lord, "Lord, I am willing to return to America if you need me."

God said, "I will use you in ways I have never used you before. I will place you before millions of people to hear you teach the Word. Your final years of ministry will be greater than the first. You will stand up strong and tall to instruct and many will listen."

"Many will listen as I give you honor among them. They will say, 'What does he have to say? He has been here a long time. He understands truth.'"

4) SPIRIT OF REBELLION

As I sat before the Lord, He said, "There will come a terrible spirit of rebellion in America."

THE SEVEN PROPHECIES GOD GAVE ME... 97

"Lord, what do you mean?" I inquired.

The greatest place you will see rebellion displayed is in the home. The home which used to be a place of tenderness and love, a place of retreat from the world to your family to laugh and play, would become a place of anger and hatred. A spirit of rebellion from the devil will come and rip the home to pieces."

If you could have been with me you would have been greatly moved as I wept and cried before God. I forgot the street scene where they were calling me a white monkey and where they were saying "go home" and "America is imperialist." I began to see Kansas City, Detroit and Pittsburgh. I saw New Orleans and Los Angeles in sadness.

I cried, "Lord, what can I do?"

The Lord said, "From coast to coast, homes will be hit like a tornado, ripped into shreds. There will be thousands of little children who must live with one parent."

"God, how can it be that homes will be torn to pieces?"

The Lord said, "Such hate will come, it will boil like a mighty wind and twist homes to pieces and divorce will be everywhere."

At this moment, a child has only a 50/50 chance of living with mom and dad together. There are second, third and fourth marriages, until children no longer know who to respect. They no longer know who to love, so they hate.

With rebellion in their hearts, they take rebellion to school. Today teachers are quitting saying, "I can't stand it anymore." The rebellion in the students against their parents, against education, against authority, against discipline, against everything that creates character, whatever creates a good person, they cannot stand it.

The Lord told me all this before it came to pass. He told me that a spirit of rebellion would attack the university campuses. The teachers would have rebellion in their hearts and would act like school children, screaming in the streets, carrying banners of rebellion.

God said that in all education a spirit of rebellion would come. He said that into the leaders of the labor movement there would be rebellion such as we had never seen before. He said rebellion would try to shut down the whole of the United States of America. He said a few men greedy for power, greedy for money, greedy for prominence would face television cameras and their names would be on the front pages of newspapers. They would be angry men seeking to drive the people into the streets like maniacs, screaming and crying, burning and turning over cars.

The same spirit in the home, in the divorce courts, in the educational institutions, in your labor movement is a spirit of rebellion in the last days!

I sat weeping at my desk in a church that I founded and built. It is the largest church in the nation. God was telling me to leave it and come home to live with you, to speak the truth out loud so people could hear it.

5) HOMOSEXUAL INVASION

Then the Lord spoke kindly into my ear, "The Americans will change in their morals."

He said, "So far, homosexuality has been practiced behind closed doors. It is a spirit that comes upon a man to cause him to lust for the body of another man." In Romans 1:24, God said that men would give themselves to uncleanness, through the lusts of their own hearts. In verse 25 it says, "Who changed the truth of God into a lie..."

Who knowing the judgment of God, that they which commit such things are worthy of death, not only do the same, but have pleasure in them that do them. (Romans 1:32)

God says that these things will come!

6) BEASTIALITY TO COME

I do not like to talk about the sixth thing God told me would come to pass. Just as you have seen homosexuals claim their rights and boast of their life style on television, the same will happen with beastiality. Women will say, "My dog is nervous and my dog can't stand it so I have to give him sex. When I give him sex, he becomes normal again." Beastiality will become a prominent sin in America and people will lay with animals. The Bible says that those who do such things are worthy of death.

> And if a man lie with a beast, he shall surely be put to death: and ye shall slay the beast. And if a woman approach unto any beast, and lie down thereto, thou shalt kill the woman, and the beast: they shall surely be put to death; their blood shall be upon them. (Leviticus 20:15-16)

7) THE HOME OF AMERICA

As I wept like Daniel in Babylon, the Lord said, "Son, you will witness the mightiest revival the human race has ever had."

This revival is described in Acts 2:17-18:

> And it shall come to pass in the last days, saith God, I will pour out of my Spirit upon all flesh:

and your sons and your daughters shall prophesy, and your young men shall see visions, and your old men shall dream dreams:

And on my servants and on my handmaidens I will pour out in those days of my Spirit; and they shall prophesy.

In these last days a revival such as no living person has witnessed will come to our generation.

For this reason I am deeply involved in television. I seek more stations to get the Full Gospel to more cities. It is one thing to be on a TV station an hour a day and then having the devil on for the rest of the day, but it is another thing for God to control the station 24 hours a day.

God said there will be a mighty outpouring of His Spirit upon our sons and our daughters. The old men and the young men shall all have an outpouring of His Spirit.

You must decide which group to be a part of; whether you choose dead "churchianity" and denominationalism which does not believe in the miraculous, or say, "I want the anointing of God, the greatest power available."

The circle will soon be complete back to the original Pentecostal rain in Acts. The former rain and the latter rain shall come at the same time and we will have a double portion of the mighty power of the Living God.

10

I PREDICT:

2000 A.D.
A GOLDEN JUBILEE
OF PLANET EARTH

The year 2000 A.D. will be the golden jubilee of planet Earth.

A jubilee is 50 years.

In Israel's history, the jubilee was celebrated by forgiving all debts and releasing every slave.

The golden jubilee, the 120th, will occur after 6000 years of human history.

This momentous point in history will coincide with the seventieth jubilee of the Israeli calendar, which dates to 1500 B.C. (the time of Noah's grandson, Nimrod).

Seven is God's number of completion; for example, God completed the entire creation in six days and rested on the seventh day.

It is significant that we have come to the seventieth jubilee; it is a year marking the complete freedom of the nation of Israel.

Throughout her hectic history, Israel has experienced dispersion, bondage, hatred, and devastation.

In the year of 1948, Israel was reborn as a nation brought back from one hundred lands and cultures. However, Israel has lived in a constant state of war throughout her new life.

The golden jubilee will mark Israel's final freedom from slavery and debt as Jesus Christ Himself establishes His throne in the Holy City.

This total fulfillment will be celebrated before or by the fateful year of 2000 A.D. The Lord Jesus said that Jerusalem shall be trodden down of the Gentiles until the time of the Gentiles is fulfilled. Possibly the time of the Gentiles began its termination period with World War I in 1914.

Planet Earth has known war from that time until today. From July 28, 1914, (the day World War I began in Austria) to January 16, 1920 (the day the League of Nations was born) is exactly 666 days multiplied by 3. This was when modern man sought to build his own tower to heaven. The League of Nations believed there would never be war again if they could get the nations together. The League of Nations became a power on the face of the earth.

Fifteen times 666 days brings you to December 7th of 1941 (the day when Japan attacked the United States at Pearl Harbor and our part in World War II began).

Seventeen of these periods of 666 days brings you to the date in 1945 when the first atomic bomb was dropped and World War II came to its termination.

Nineteen times 666 brings you to March 18, 1949, when the North Atlantic pact brought America and the European nations together to fight against Communism.

Then if you take 21 times the 666 day period, you will come to November of 1952, when the "hell bomb," nitrogen bomb, was tested and exploded.

In the Bible the year 50 is the jubilee year.

When you finish the 49 years of man, you come to God's jubilee. If you multiply man's part of this (49 x 666), you will discover that is 32,634 days from World War I. It would come on June 1, 2002. At that time Jesus Christ shall rule over planet Earth for 1000 years!

The 50th year was the year when all men went free and debts were automatically cancelled. This will be fulfilled in the Millennium! None of us will be in debt during the Millennium and everyone shall have plenty.

What excites me is that mathematically the year 2000 is the turnaround for planet Earth! We have reached the Saturday night of mankind! A thousand years is a day and a day is a thousand years. We have now come to the glorious illuminated Sabbath. The Sabbath day was the day of rest for Elohim. The thousand-year reign of Christ will be the day of rest for all humanity! In Luke 21:24, Jesus said that foreigners would rule Jerusalem until the time of the Gentiles is finished. I believe the time of the Gentiles has actually died. The perilous times of our hour reveal the death knell of Gentile rule.

THE DOOMSDAY CLOCK

There are exciting signs regarding the year 2000 A.D. A magazine published by scientists places on the front page of each issue the hands of a clock positioned by world tensions. In each edition the hands are set at six minutes to twelve, or five minutes to twelve, or three minutes to twelve. When there is relative peace they move the hands of Doomsday back to six to twelve midnight. The hands have been down to one minute to twelve! This means the scientists thought the end of the world was certainly close.

It is amazing that so few people realize the destiny of today. Many people do not understand the times in which they live. They are too involved with personal problems.

While good people are involved in their own problems, the enemy is destroying homes and lives. The Church is so involved with its own problems that it does not have time to pray. We do not have time to look at our neighbors and search to see what we can do to save America.

I feel sure the whole destiny of planet Earth will be resolved before A.D. 2000!

We have so many amazing signs in our times

regarding the return of the Lord Jesus. Some of them are beautiful things like radio and television. Job 38:35 says about the Lord, "Canst thou send lightnings, (that is radio and television) that they may go, and say unto thee, Here we are?"

Many years ago God knew the time would come when we would speak to planet Earth saying, "Here we are! God is real!"

Our shortwave station is touching one-fourth of the human race. It reaches one hundred nations. Amazing things are going to take place until this whole world shall be enveloped with the Gospel of Jesus Christ and everyone who wants to be saved will be saved by the power of God!

Prophecy related to television is described in Revelation 11:9,

> And they of the people and kindreds and tongues and nations shall see their dead bodies three days and a half, and shall not suffer their dead bodies to be put in graves.

Although the book of Revelation was written almost 2000 years ago, it states that nations, kingdoms and peoples shall see the bodies of the two witnesses of God who were witnessing during the Great Tribulation. All nations shall see them lying in the streets of Jerusalem! The Antichrist will be so angry with them that he will not permit their bodies to be picked up off the street.

The power of the Holy Ghost will come upon those men and they will rise up before the television cameras. The entire world shall see these two witnesses of God rise up three days after their execution.

As these men praise and magnify God, no doubt millions of people throughout the earth will fall on their faces and say, "We have never seen this before."

One of the remarkable signs in the cosmos indicating that Jesus is coming soon is in nature. Jesus said in Luke 21:11, "And great earthquakes shall be in divers places..."

Our neighboring country, Mexico, was shaken and mighty buildings began to disintegrate and fall to the ground. When you pick up a newspaper and read about an earthquake in some part of the world, you may not pay too much attention to it if it is in Afghanistan, India, or Africa. But when the quakes hit close to home, we get scared.

Recently the scientists found a second fault near the San Andreas Fault down the center of California. They said that the second one was worse than the first.

Some may say, "But we have always had earthquakes."

In the 16th century there were 115.

In the 17th century there were 253.

In the 18th century there were 378.

In the 19th century there were 640.

In the 20th century there have already been more than 2119.

What a jump from 640 to 2119!

God is trying to get our attention.

I assure you that from this moment on toward 2000 A.D., men are going to understand less and less about sin. They are going to cover up for sin and make excuses for sins.

In your heart you must speak hard against sin. You must teach your children against sin. You must show them how dreadful it is to sin.

It is wonderful to me that Noah was able to keep his family from sinning while he was building the ark.

Probably the whole dirty bunch of sinners in Noah's town danced around the ark every night. It was probably the dancing spot where they made illicit love and did all kinds of sinful things. However, Noah was able to keep his sons and his daughters-in-law from sin. They walked into the ark clean and pure before God!

Parents today must live the kind of life Noah lived to be able to guide their families.

I am not telling you that Jesus will not return until 2000 A.D. He could return today. I am saying that we are nearing the end of the sixth day. We are in the Saturday night of time; Sunday morning is upon us. Sunday morning will be the Sabbath, which speaks to us of the millennial reign of the Lord Jesus.

I beg you to prepare for the coming of the Lord. Do not let the devil deceive you. The riches of this world are not eternal. If you become a multimillionaire, of what eternal value is it to you? You can only eat one meal, wear one suit, drive one car, live in one house, and sleep in one bed. The exceedingly rich cannot do any more than that. Riches can get you into a lot of trouble, if you start worshiping wealth rather than worshiping God. You can even miss heaven because of wealth.

Remember: I predict 2000 A.D. to be the ultimate day of destiny for planet Earth!

YOU, TOO, CAN BE SAVED!

I ask you: If you're not born again, if you are not *sure* where you'd go if you were to die RIGHT NOW, please ask Jesus into your heart. He will give you peace, and joy, and hope!

You need a personal Savior, a personal commitment to Him who is able and willing to forgive you of ALL your sins. Pray this Sinner's Prayer, and really MEAN it.

"Lord Jesus, I am a sinner. I believe that you died and rose from the tomb to save me from my sins. Forgive me by Your grace for all the sins that I have committed. Wash me with Your blood, and I shall be clean. I ask You into my heart right <u>now</u>. Be my Savior and my guide forever. Amen."

In your flesh, you may not FEEL any different. But, the Word of God tells us that you are now a New Creature, and old things are passed away and forgiven. You are no longer under condemnation. You are in Christ Jesus and you now walk after the Spirit,(Romans 8:1, II Corinthians 5:17, I John 2:12, Luke 7:47)

Now that you have become a child of God, please write and I will send you a little pamphlet titled "So You're Born Again!"

Write to: **Lester Sumrall Box 12, South Bend, Indiana 46624.**

Other books by Lester Sumrall:

- My Story To His Glory
- Take It—It's Yours
- Gifts & Ministries Of The Holy Spirit
- Conscience—The Scales Of Eternal Justice
- Demons The Answer Book
- Bitten By Devils
- Ecstasy—Finding Joy In Living
- Faith To Change The World
- Faith Under Siege; The Life of Abraham
- Fishers Of Men
- Genesis—Crucible Of The Universe
- Grief—You Can Conquer It
- Hostility
- Imagination—Hidden Force Of Human Potential
- I Predict 2000 A.D.
- Jerusalem, Where Empires Die—
     Will America Die At Jerusalem?
- Jihad—The Holy War
- Living Free
- Making Life Count
- Miracles Don't Just Happen
- 101 Questions & Answers On Demon Power
- Paul—Man Of The Millennia
- Run With The Vision
- Supernatural Principalities & Powers
- 20 Years Of "I Predict"
- The Will—The Potent Force Of The Universe
- The Battle Of The Ages
- The Total Man
- The Human Body
- The Human Soul
- The Human Spirit
- Unprovoked Murder
- Miracles And The Sumrall Family
  (by Leona Sumrall Murphy)
- The Marriage Triangle (Leona Sumrall Murphy)

Imagination, Hidden Force of Human Potential

Imagination gives birth to empires, fortunes, art, music, literature, architecture, and new inventions. Imagination is a tremendous force—it is creative in becoming the person Christ wants you to be.

How To Know – THE WILL OF GOD

How can I find God's will for my life?
You can know God's will by listening to His voice. Walk in His Word as He has identified it to you. Then when God says do something, just do it!

Conscience, The Eternal Scales of Justice

Your conscience is a watchman over your soul. This generation has a conscience burned out as by a hot iron, and many people do not know right from wrong.

Each book: REG. $1.95   **NOW $1.49**